NEVER LET THEM BE

SO LOST

THAT EVEN THE

ANGELS ARE UNABLE

TO FIND THEM!

ROLE MODELS

Tracey Connelly was born Tracey Cox on June 29, 1981, in the East Midlands town of Leicester to her mother, Irish born Mary O'Connor, known as Nula to her friends and Gary Cox, a delivery driver by trade. Gary was the man Tracey regarded as her father, until the age of 12 when a drunken Mary, casually informed her daughter she was, in fact, the product of a drunken one-night stand in Leicester with a married family friend named Richard Johnson. Johnson was a convicted pedophile who raped a teenager in the Midlands in the 1970s and was convicted of another sex offence in the 1980s. Gary, an alcoholic and habitual drug user, paid Richard five pounds in what he thought was a funny joke, to sleep with Mary. Richard, a jobless gardener, drunk at the time, took up his offer as he was going through a bad patch with his own wife, but later said it was something he regretted for the rest of his life. More often than not drunk, Gary used to subject Mary to regular, vicious beatings, blaming her for the house being filthy among other things. He regularly laid into her with his bare fists and the beatings were so violent that the family pet dog ran away in fear. He never hit the children, but tried to turn them against their mother, saying, "She's evil. Don't listen to her."

Tracey was brought up in a house where violence was the norm and grew up in a household where beatings were a daily ritual. Alcohol and drugs were part of everyday life. The marriage break up of Tracey's parents was inevitable and Mary escaped Gary's beatings and abuse and moved her and the one year old Tracey to a tough council estate in North London. Gary, who would later die of a heart attack at the age of 44 when Tracey was seven years old, in 1998, was left behind to drink his life away. Life was not to get any better for Tracey, growing up in the poverty of a rundown council flat in the tough unforgiving ghetto of

Islington, North London. Mary, by now a bone thin, haggard woman who stood out in her trade mark leggings, socks and stiletto heels turned increasingly to alcohol and drugs as a means of getting her through the day. The flat they lived in was filthy, with dog excrement left on the kitchen floor by their uncared for black mongrel dog. Unwashed clothes were strewn in every room, there was very little furniture, and there were never any sheets on the beds. By the time Tracey started to attend primary school, she was overweight and due to her mother's neglect, always looked dirty and scruffy in her unwashed thread bare clothes and unwashed hair. She would turn up at school in shoes that were falling apart and ripped tracksuit bottoms. The other children soon gave her the nickname 'Tracey the Tramp' because of her appearance and she was often the victim of beatings from other pupils and returned home on more than one occasion with a split lip and bruises. She was the kid at school no one wanted to play with and away from school had very few friends or social contact with others. She was later to describe her childhood on her Facebook page simply as 'Shitty'.

Mary came from a violent and abusive background herself, a pattern she continued with her own children. Records from Leicestershire and Islington social services showed the grandmother had a violent upbringing and was violent to her own children. Records stated that she admitted hitting her son from the age of six weeks, accepted she had a problem with violence particularly against men, and was convicted of the malicious wounding of her husband. Her own son was admitted to the hospital four times by the time he was three years old, although each accident was regarded as having an adequate explanation.

Tracey soon started to develop a tough veneer. Always alone and hanging around by herself she soon learned to put up or shut up. A neighbor recalled how Tracey used to come to her door and say it was her birthday, and she would give Tracey a fiver. She would then remember it was her birthday last week too. Mary was by now spending most of her time in bed smoking cannabis with an assortment of different boyfriends or casual lovers and would often shout at Tracey to clear out of the flat. Tracey was left to wander the streets of North London, alone, late at night. It was around this time that Tracey complained to her mother that she, herself, was being abused by a close male relative. Her mother's reaction was to shout and scream at her and call her a liar. Lonely, fatherless, and lacking any self-esteem, she went in search of whatever affection she could find.

As young as eleven, Tracey was promiscuous and was known as easy by the youngsters on the estate. She spent her evenings with an assortment of different local lads who would take her into dark alleys or the stairwells of the flats and have their way with her, without showing any love or affection, only to call her names behind her back and let others know where to find 'an easy lay'. She also began to spend a lot of time in the flat of a man in his 60s who used to give her beer and cigarettes and was seen by friends play wrestling and kissing her on the neck. Exactly what went on up there is not known but it was not a healthy environment for a girl of her age. With family relationships reaching their breaking point in the Cox home, Tracey said that the revelations about her real father drove her 'a bit wild' for a time, until Islington social services became involved. A place was found for Tracey, aged 12, at Farney Close boarding school in West Sussex, an institution catering to children with special education needs and behavioral and social problems.

Farney Close is rated as 'outstanding' by Ofsted, the school rating organization, and described by many former pupils, who include Olympic athlete Daley Thompson, as 'brilliant', boasting facilities to rival a top private school. This could have been the chance for Tracey to escape her childhood. Instead, 'Tracey the Tramp' was given a new nickname, 'Stig', short for 'Stig of the Dump', the character out of a children's book, where Stig lived in a rubbish dump.

One former pupil, now a 27-year-old chef, recalled how she was dirty, scruffy and her feet stank. Her personal hygiene was very poor. She would only shower once a week when told to, her face was greasy and covered in acne, and she was still overweight. Tracey's time at Farney Close could have been a chance for Tracey to turn her life into something different from the abuse and misery she had suffered, but she couldn't be bothered to make any effort. She used to wear Dr Marten boots or boys' shoes because her feet were so large, size ten, and only ever wore trousers. She also showed that she had a real temper on her, and would often get into fights with other pupils who regarded her as a lazy oddball. On more than one occasion she had to be restrained by a teacher after getting into a fight with another pupil.

At Farney Close, a whole range of sports were available including go-karting and canoeing, that Tracey had the opportunity to learn and participate in, but Tracey preferred to watch TV soap operas and lay in bed. The only arena where she excelled was on the netball court, where her size made her an effective goalkeeper. While alcohol and drugs were banned at the school, pupils were allowed to smoke with their parents' consent and, needless to say, Tracey chain-smoked. Despite her scruffy and dirty appearance, Tracey was never without a boyfriend and was always seen during the school holidays back home in North London with someone new by her side. She left Farney Close with a handful of GCSEs and vague ideas about being a hairdresser, but, as she told her best friend at school, what she really wanted was a 'houseful of kids'.

At the age of 16, she met her first serious boyfriend, a railway worker, 17 years her senior and it looked like finally Tracey was settling into a normal life. Within two years they had moved in together and Tracey became pregnant with her first baby, a girl, and a second baby girl soon followed. They married in a civil ceremony in

Haringey in September 2003; with Tracey dressed in a plunging black dress with an ill matching white veil and him in a suit. Her wedding pictures show her belting out a karaoke song, a glass of her favorite vodka and Coke in hand, and guests said the couple sang the Sonny and Cher duet 'I Got You Babe'. Their reception was held at a pub in north London, but their relationship was not to be a lasting union. A third baby girl was born shortly after the wedding. Together they had moved into a council house in Tottenham and it looked like her dream of a household full of kids was coming true.

Old habits die hard and Tracey wasn't the cleanest mother in the world and wasn't bothered if the kids were dirty. You would have thought with the abuse she suffered from her own appearance as a child, she would have made an extra effort to make sure her own children did not suffer the same fate, but the children were always dirty and clad in unwashed clothes. The house was a mess and very rarely cleaned or tidy. Her husband would come home to no meal prepared and no housework done. Regular arguments and fights were had because of Tracey's laziness and lack of general household skills. On one occasion, she hit her daughter in front of the school nurse, because her daughter had claimed she was being molested and when Tracey went up to the school to sort it out, she found out she'd made it up. Things calmed down in the household when Tracey found out she was pregnant with her fourth child.

There was nothing unusual in the circumstances of the new baby's birth on 1 March 2006, at the North Middlesex Hospital in Edmonton, north London, to suggest his life was destined to be brutal and tragically short. The North Mid, as the hospital is known, had long since cast off its workhouse origins. Its children's facilities, run as they are by specialists from the world renowned Great Ormond Street Hospital, are first rate. The baby was born, at least, in good hands. His mother, just short of her 25th birthday, and his father had finally been blessed with a much-wanted son after three daughters. Their family appeared complete. The baby was named Peter and with blonde hair and blue eyes looked like a little angel. His first hospital visit of many to come was to be weighed and treated for nappy rash. With cigarettes and vodka to buy, Tracey had no money left to spend on such things as lotion for the baby. On May 2nd, Peter made his first trip to see his local general practitioner, suffering from vomiting and was prescribed a medicine to ease his stomach.

The joy of a new baby boy and the complete family was short-lived. The couple's relationship was on the rocks. Tracey spent most of her time either flirting or meeting strange men from internet social networking sites. The house was unkempt and her constant drinking, smoking and infidelity was too much for her husband to take, so on July 17, 1986, the children's father left Tracey. He moved out after Tracey decided to take Steven Barker with her to a school reunion instead of her husband. She became so obsessed with him she had his initials tattooed on to her back.

Tracey was not on living on her own for long. In February, 2007, Tracey moved in to a new housing association property in Harringey with the children and her new boyfriend, 33 year old Steven Barker, the man her husband had accused her of being unfaithful with, and who she had met while he was doing maintenance work on her neighbor's flat before baby Peter was born.

TRACEY CONNELLY IN HER USUAL POSITION ON HER COMPUTER

THE BROTHERS GRIM

Steven Barker moved in with new girlfriend, Tracey Connelly, in her new home on Penshurst Road, without the authorities or social services knowing. Connelly used all her guile to hide his presence from the authorities. As a single mother-of-four, she had no intention of losing her £450 monthly benefit or the allowance paid by her ex-husband.

Friends of Tracey's said the new relationship appeared to be good for her and that she seemed happy and settled for the first time in a while. Online, she boasted how great it was to be "in love". Steven, who appeared at first to be the perfect boyfriend, had an unsavory past of his own. At six feet four inches, and 18 stones (252 lbs.), Barker was a big, powerful man. He was born in 1976, and brought up in Totenham, London. He was the second eldest of five siblings, three boys and two girls. Even as a young child he started to show signs of sadistic behavior, when he would torture guinea pigs and frogs, which he would skin alive before breaking their legs and making the agonized creatures hop. He was prosecuted by the Royal Society for the Prevention of Cruelty to Animals (RSPCA) for his torture of animals.

Barker was sent to a school for children with learning difficulties near his childhood home in North London and was barely able to read and write. He had an IQ of just 60 and was described by people who knew him as 'simple'. Often suffering from dark moods and depression, he would lock himself in a room for days. He underwent medical treatment for depression but preferred to use his taste for torture to lift himself out of his dark moods. The sinister side of Steven Barker started to show itself again when neighbors watched different groups of men entering his flat in Haringey, believing he was holding secret meetings with racists and neo Nazis from the fascist National Front, they were always weary about Barker. He and his brother were later investigated for committing race crimes against an Asian family in the area, but no charges were brought against them. He started to collect Nazi memorabilia; including swastika decorated helmets and daggers as well as taking an interest in the survivalist movement and martial arts. Among his prized possessions were a crossbow and various lethal martial arts weapons and would often stride around the house in his combat gear.

Barker prided himself on his ability to live 'rough' and would disappear for days on end in Epping Forest, catching rabbits and skinning them to eat with his beloved Rottweiler dog Kaiser, named after the German First World War leader. Despite his size, Barker had been abused as a youngster at the hands of his older brother Jason Owen, who had the nickname 'fatboy' as a child. Jason would terrorize, bully and beat his younger brother. Owen used to have the same surname as Steven but changed it after a family argument. Steven and Jason's sister, Susan, said that Steven Barker was petrified of their brother Jason. During one occasion, she was walking past their flat and saw Steven at the window looking scared, with Jason behind him. A few days later, she saw Steven and he had cigarette burns all over his hands.

Steven's fear of Jason did not stop the teenage brothers from teaming up and terrorizing their grandmother in the pursuit of money. Barker and Owen would often visit their grandmother in the seaside town of Whitstable, Kent. In November 1995, when Barker was aged 19 and Owen was 23, the pair repeatedly attacked their grandmother Hilda Barker over her will. On one occasion, they locked her in a wardrobe and shook it over and over again in an attempt to get her to change her will in their favor. Jacqueline Cole, Mrs. Barker's neighbor recalls that Hilda was terrified every time they arrived and would see bruises on the old lady after they had left. Mrs. Cole's husband, David, saw the brothers take axes, spades and shovels from the couple's garden and said he feared they used the tools to threaten the terrified woman. Too proud or too ashamed, Hilda never told Mrs. Cole what the boys had done to her. On another occasion, they wore Guy Fawkes masks in an attempt to scare her and on at least one occasion beat her up all in pursuit of becoming the heirs to her money.

Hilda Barker dreaded the visits from her grandsons and she was so frightened by their constant threats and abuse that she ended up moving into a care home to get away from their harassment. Jason and Steven were arrested after Mrs. Barker's daughter called the police. They were charged with grievous bodily harm but before the case could come to court, Mrs. Barker, who by now was in the care home, died of pneumonia, in January 1996. With their main witness dead and with no medical evidence to support a manslaughter or attempted murder charge, Kent Police dropped the case, a decision which is said to have stunned detectives from the Metropolitan Police when they read the case files at a later date.

A Kent Police spokesman said, "In 1995, Kent Police were contacted by relatives of an 82-year-old lady living in Whitstable. It was suggested that other members of her family had assaulted her. The allegations were investigated and, although two males were charged over the alleged attack, the matter was later discontinued through lack of admissible evidence. In January 1996 the lady died and an inquest concluded her death was as a result of pneumonia, of natural causes. The coroner did say, however, that this attack hadn't helped the woman."All this happened more than a decade before Barker met Tracey Connelly and whether she was aware of his past is unknown.

Jason Owen, born in February 1972, was the eldest of the children in the Barker household and was four years older than Steven. From an early age Owen liked to bully his younger siblings. He was often in trouble and at the young age of 13, he was accused of raping an 11 year old girl. Police investigated claims that he had beaten and bullied the terrified young girl before carrying out the sex attack. The case was dropped for lack of evidence, due to the age of the victim, but this close call did not teach Owen any life lessons and he continued to commit crimes. By the time Owen was 20 years old, he had already amassed a long criminal record, with convictions for theft and burglary and was also convicted of carrying offensive weapons. When he was 16, he was arrested and taken to court for stealing and burglary, for which he was convicted, fined, and put on probation. When he was arrested again at the age of 20 for carrying the offensive weapon, he was again fined.

Owen managed to stay out of trouble for the following years, or at least avoided getting caught, in which time he married, fathered five children and became addicted to crack cocaine. He was also involved in racist activities with the National Front, along with his brother. The drug addiction was his next excuse for breaking the law when he was again caught and convicted of burglary twice; he needed money to feed his drug habit. It is also know that Owen robbed and preyed on the vulnerable and robbed pensioners. Things were to take a more sinister twist when Owen was arrested for arson when he set fire to his own house to try and claim the insurance money. He was convicted and jailed for arson. Arson was again the theme of his threats when five years later he was investigated for threatening to kill his sister and telling her he was going to set fire to her house. The police never pursued the threats made against his sister, as the threats stopped. His sister described him as aggressive and violent and told of how he used to torture animals, beat his brothers, and stated he was a bully and a wife beater. He often hit his ex wife, and on one occasion beat her with a red hot iron.

STEVEN BARKER

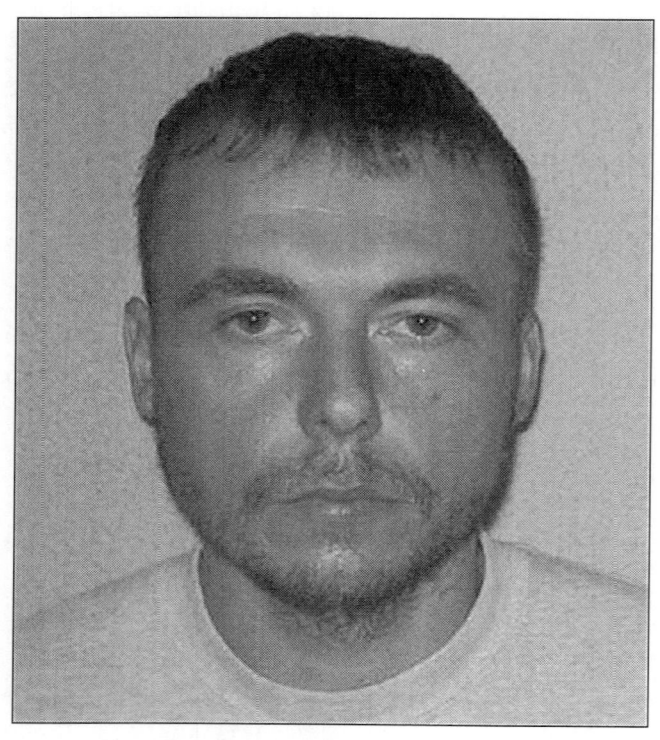

JASON (BARKER) OWEN

THE HOUSE OF SQUALOUR

It did not take Tracey Connelly long after moving into her new house with her children and Steven Barker to revert to her old ways. Housework was not a word she was familiar with and the house was soon the filthy mess she was accustomed to. The floors were dirty with dog mess left from her German Shepherd, 'Lady', and her Staffordshire Bull Terrier called 'Lucky'. Far more attention was lavished on the dogs than was given to her children, who were left for hours unattended while Tracey spent her days and evenings chain smoking in a fume filled room while drinking vodka and lager, whilst laying on the sofa, or stuck in front of her computer or the television watching American crime dramas such as CSI. When not watching television, she would spend hours talking on social networking sites and watching pornography while the house degenerated into a slum. On the social networking site, Bebo, she wrote, "My life is crazy. Have moved house and I'm loving my new place. My fella is nuts but being in love is great."

In the house, Steven Barker kept two pet snakes which he fed with rats, mice and chickens. Dead rodents and the remains of butchered chickens were left to rot in the filthy kitchen. The place was infested with fleas and stank of stale urine but this did not bother Tracey or Barker who were far more involved in their perverse pursuits to care about the state of the house or the welfare of the children inside it. Although Tracey described her new baby, Peter, on one internet site as "the coolest person I have ever met", that feeling was not to last long. Barker, when not playing with his snakes, would lavish all his affection on his pet Rottweiler dog, which he adored. He would often complain to Tracey about the disgusting state of the house, but did not bother to clean up after himself or his pets. Nazi memorabilia and weapons were left casually around the house including a selection of knives, crossbows and axes.

Sex was one of things that mattered most to Tracey, who once wrote on a social networking site, "It's funny when you meet someone and fall in love. You spend as much time as possible kissing and touching and having sex. You want to make them feel so good you just can't get enough of each other. It's great." The honeymoon period of happiness between Connelly and Barker did not last for long. Stomping around in his army pants, he started to call Connelly fat and ugly among other names. Inside him, was welling up a resentment towards baby Peter because he had been fathered by a different man. He already had a child from another relationship who he never saw and wanted a baby of his own with Tracey. When Peter was learning to speak he was taught to call Barker 'dad' but this just reminded Barker that he was not the real father and the resentment grew. He taught Peter to give a Nazi 'seig heil' salute and say "Heil Hitler" when he entered the room to boost his own ego and pander to his love of all things Nazi. Peter just craved any sort of attention and love and would innocently oblige in the hope he would be showed just a single crumb of affection.

Tracey Connelly's real father, Richard Johnson, occasionally popped round to see his daughter and grandchildren and he was shocked by what he saw, but says he didn't feel it was his place to 'interfere'. After all, social services might have questioned his presence there, for Richard Johnson had an unsavory past of his own, with the conviction for the rape of a 14-year-old during the

1970s. He said the house was a cesspit and called his daughter bone idle, but did not step up to the mark and do anything to change or help his grandchildren from the disgusting conditions they were living in. He witnessed Peter giving Nazi salutes and saw firsthand the filth the children had to endure, a mixture of human and dog excrement, rubbed into the carpet.

Peter was first referred to the child abuse investigation team on December 12, 2006, even before Barker moved in, after being admitted to Whittington Hospital in North London with bruising to his forehead, nose, breastbone and right shoulder. He had a prior visit to the hospital on Friday, October 13th to see the doctor with a bruised head and chest. Tracey had told the doctor he had fallen over. When Dr. Ikwueke saw bruising on the side of the infant's head and chest and asked how it had happened, the mother told him that Baby Peter had fallen down the stairs. Almost one month later, when Dr Ikwueke examined him again, Baby Peter had a bulging 2 inch bruise in the middle of his forehead as well as bruising on his chest and right shoulder. Concerned by his mother's unclear explanation for the injuries, she suggested they might have occurred while he was being cared for by his grandmother. The doctor referred Tracey and Peter to a specialist at the Whittington Hospital in north London. Dr Heather Mackinnon, the specialist who examined him the following day, was so disturbed by his condition she referred him to Haringey social services

Both Connelly and her own abusive mother, who used to mind the children, were arrested and questioned on Dec 19th, although no charges were ever filed. Peter was put on Haringey Council's child protection register three days later. Tracey used to say Peter was accident prone and kept bumping into things. Peter had a few weeks of the care and attention he so badly craved and needed while in the care of a family friend while social services and Police investigated. The woman who looked after him for six weeks over Christmas 2006 noted that he did not get any more bruises and ate and slept well. However, she reported that he would head-butt, scratch and bite. His mother continued to have extensive access to him. During this period, social workers visited seven times in two weeks, including an unannounced visit to check on him. The very same authorities were to let him down so badly in the start of a series of unforgiveable mistakes, mishandling and total incompetence.

At the end of six weeks, despite the continuing police investigation and numerous visits, social services remained unaware that the mother's boyfriend was living in the house. Social workers returned Peter home despite the house being a disgusting mess, flea ridden and smelling of urine. Barker was still being concealed, as not to affect Connelly's precious benefits. This was only one of what would turn out to be more than 60 visits to the household by Haringey's totally inept authorities. On top of Barker living there when he was not supposed to, the brother who bullied and beat him when they were younger, and who he still feared, moved into the small house whilst on the run from the police. He brought with him his underage, runaway girlfriend, who was just 15 years of age, and four of his children from his previous marriage would regularly stay there. It was around this time that Jason Barker changed his surname to Owen, later stating it was because of a family argument, but it is more likely he did it as a means of avoiding capture from the police. Still the authorities remained unaware that there were now two extra adults, a runaway teenager, and three extra children along with Connelly and her own children and three dogs, two of them classed as dangerous animals to be around children, all living in this squalid environment of the Penshurst Road house.

Professionals continued to monitor the family regularly, sometimes two or three times a week. The longest period the children went without contact with at least one professional was 10 days. Social services only made two unannounced visits between January 2007 and Baby Peter's death eight months later. During that period, Dr. Ikwueke again noticed bruising on the baby's face and despite the mother's explanation that he had been pushed into a fireplace by another child, he referred the infant to a senior doctor at the North Middlesex. That doctor described how, when he examined him, the 13-month-old child was holding his head to one side and was unsteady on his feet. He was admitted to the hospital overnight, but released the next day.

Social workers continued to visit. They believed Peter was an 'active child', who was seen to throw his body around and head-butt family members and other objects. These appeared to support the mother's concerns that her son suffered frequent accidents due to being an active, clumsy child with a high pain threshold. They concentrated on discovering if there were 'organic reasons for such behaviour' instead of investigating further. The mother's two elder daughters did not give cause for concern. Despite questions of lack of hygiene and unkemptness, both attended school regularly. Sources close to Haringey Council later told lawyers their main concern was one of neglect and poor parenting skills rather than abuse. They remained unaware of the boyfriend's presence in the house. On one of only two occasions when social workers turned up without invitation, they discovered more bruising and scratching on Peter. He was immediately examined by a senior doctor at the North Middlesex Hospital who found multiple bruises. Four days later, his mother was interviewed under caution at Hornsey police station. Detectives visited the house to photograph Peter's injuries and the furniture he was said to have collided with. Social workers placed the eldest daughter on the child protection register.

Somehow, the Barkers presence in Peter's home remained undetected throughout this investigation. It wasn't until

June 15th that Marie Lockhart, a Haringey family support worker, was introduced to a tall blond man whom Connelly described as a "friend". It was the first time that anyone in authority appeared to learn of his existence. More astonishing, perhaps, is the fact that not only did the boyfriend's presence in the home remain unknown for so long, but so did that of Jason Owen and his brood. Connelly later claimed she had asked Owen and the others to leave but they had refused. A friend said the mother was unhappy with the situation and 'frightened of Owen'. Despite this, she did not mention her fears to anyone in authority.

THE FILTHY SQUALID HOUSE ON PENSHURST ROAD

A FULL HOUSE OF HORROR

Tracey Connelly sat at her computer, as usual, but this time not to boast how in love she was because her relationship with Barker had gone pear shaped. In a familiar vein to when she was younger and nicknamed 'Tracey Tramp', she had to listen to daily abuse and name calling from her boyfriend. Feeling sorry for herself and full of self-pity, she wrote on one social networking site, "I'm fed up with letting people down. All my life I have messed up. When will I ever get it right? People should stay away from me as I have always messed up everyone who's close to me. I'm a jinx to all I know."

Baby Peter was now being left in his cot upstairs until mid afternoon, unchanged and unfed and when he was brought downstairs he spent most of his time in his playpen, apart from the times Barker would take him out to play his new games, games that were for his own amusement, not Peter's. One of his favorites was to place Peter on a rotating stool and spin him as hard and fast as he could until he fell off, or he would take him off so he would stagger and fall into furniture or on the wretched, stained floor. Aware but unconcerned, Connelly continued to loaf on the sofa drinking and watching TV, or sat in her other seat in front of the computer screen. On February 22nd, Maria Ward was appointed as the family's social worker. On her first visit to the flea infested house on March 2nd, an unclean Peter was crawling around the carpet and she made a note that he spent time head butting the wall, but noted it was a possible sign of a 'development problem' instead of a cry for help. Maria Ward was the allocated social worker for 18 different child protection cases at the time, flouting Haringey Council's own recommendations that its social workers should only be responsible for a maximum of 12 children.

Owen also started to join in the daily routine of shoving and punching Peter in what Barker later described as "exercises to toughen the lad up". The torture and cruelty inflicted on Peter steadily got worse, but still Tracey Connelly was unmoved and not at all bothered by what was going on. In March, Connelly gave a recorded interview to social worker, Sue Gilmore. In the interview, Connelly claimed her son Peter, then 12 months old, had 'banged his chin' by accident at a friend's house. She said she comforted him immediately afterwards and then took pictures of the table on which he 'caught himself' as evidence to prove she was innocent. Although she revealed that her sadistic boyfriend, Steven Barker, was spending time in her home with the toddler, no further checks were carried out and details of the interview were not entered fully on case files.

Had social workers looked into Barker's background, they would have discovered he had been questioned by police on suspicion of torturing his grandmother and prosecuted by the RSPCA for abusing animals. The details should have set alarm bells ringing and could have saved the youngster's life. Throughout the interview, Mrs Gilmore, a senior team manager in the social work department at Haringey, appeared eager to accept Connelly's explanations for her son's injuries and when Connelly said she wished social workers would 'back off and leave me alone' she sympathized, saying that was a 'straightforward thing to want' She recorded the hour-long interview as part of a course in new social work methods aimed at encouraging parents to cooperate with the authorities. She failed the training assignment and did not complete the course.

At the end of the interview, she said, "I'm impressed, really, really impressed with the way you have been able to come in here, sit in front of that (pointed to the camera)". Connelly denied she was in a relationship with Barker, but then said, "He is 6ft 4in, blond hair, green eyes and I am sorry if I've built up a dreamboat on him but he is every girl's dream." She added, "I don't like having people interfere. I know that the social worker is there for a job, and I know they are there for a purpose and at the end of all this I hope they will back off and leave me alone so that I am a caring mother. Does that make sense?"

THE SMILING SOCIAL WORKER LISTENS TO CONNELLY'S LIES

On March 22nd, Maria Ward made another visit to the house. The small army of people now living there had made themselves scarce for the day. Maria noticed a strange red mark on Peter's chin and when she asked Connelly how it happened she replied, "Peter had fallen over a table". In her notes Maria wrote it down as insignificant.

Peter was either left in his cot crying for days on end or subjected to ever increasing bouts of torture. Barker was now teaching his Rottweiler dog how to bite using Peter as the goad. The dog would bite Peter while Barker and Owen would fall about in fits of laughter. Instead of objecting to her son's brutal treatment, she never showed any signs of concern or emotion. Connelly covered up and hid Peter's injuries the best she could. If Peter dared to cry, he was picked up by the throat and thrown into his cot, his windpipe pressed so hard that he turned blue. On other occasions, he had a bottled rammed into his mouth so hard it cut his lips. He was dropped on the floor from a height of six feet and punched and kicked. A neighbor noticed, on two occasions, that Peter was bleeding from his ear after Barker had bathed him. The day to day care or lack of it, of Peter, was now left solely in the hands of Barker and Owen while Connelly slouched on the sofa complaining of fatigue and depression. On April 9th, Peter was admitted to North Middlesex Hospital suffering from bruises. His mother claimed another child caused him to fall against a marble fireplace. Police were not informed. After only one of the two unannounced visits by social workers, they noticed Peter was covered in bruises and they told Connelly to take him to hospital, which she did on June 2nd.

He is taken to North Middlesex Hospital again and found to have 12 areas of bruising. Connelly is rearrested, but blamed another child for marks to Peter's face. In what would prove to be the last months of his life, Baby Peter's general condition deteriorated. A child minder noted he had become lethargic and spent more time in his playpen, but didn't want to play. His hair had been shaved in a radical attempt to curb head lice and he had extensive infections on his scalp, ears, fingers and toes. His mother continued to take him to a variety of doctors who prescribed antibiotics.

Through June the abuse got worse. In one act of savage cruelty, Barker pulled some of the baby's fingernails and toe nails out with a pair of pliers and proceeded to punch the boy in the head and face. Barker committed one of his most brutal attacks on Peter in June. He threw the child around on the sofa like a rag doll, raised the baby in the air with both hands, and slammed him against his knee with force. This took place in full view of Connelly, Owen, and Owen's fifteen year old girlfriend. The teenager later told police that Barker was smoking cannabis and drinking when he slammed the child against his knee and that the crack was so loud it echoed around the house. She also stated that Barker sat smirking as the baby let out a gut wrenching scream. It was so loud the teenager went into the garden and put her hands over her ears to block out the sound. Peter's spine had been snapped in half. The teenager was so terrified that she would be made a target as well that it took her months to summon up the courage to tell relatives of the abuse. She claimed the mother's lies about her child's various injuries were 'simply accepted' by the social workers checking up on her.

On July 27th, Peter's natural father had the child stay with him overnight. Peter was lifeless and withdrawn and he noticed the child was incredibly thin. Peter was a sorry sight, with a bandaged hand and badly infected scalp. He raised these issues with Connelly, who told him the baby had been poorly and had bit his own fingernail off. It would be the last time he would see his son alive. He had offered to care for his son at an earlier date when he thought the child was not being taken care of properly. The authorities turned him down because Connelly falsely claimed he had slapped his son. Peter might still be alive today if he had been handed over to his father, who had gotten permission to take time off work and had references of his good character from his employer. Social workers believed Connelly, who was already under investigation.

Lawyers advised Haringey council social workers, on the 25th of July, that they could not legally take Peter into care. Haringey's Children and Young Persons Service presented all the evidence it had collated to the council's legal department. Lawyers told the social workers that "on the basis of the information provided, the threshold for initiating care proceedings ... was not met." The same month, police finished their enquiries into the injuries Peter sustained in December 2006 and June 2007. Detectives said their efforts had proved inconclusive and no criminal charges would be brought.

Social Worker, Maria Ward, was due for a pre arranged visit on the 30th of July. Peter had bruises covering his body, head, and face. His lips were cut, eyes dark, and he had scabs and scratches on his scalp. His back was broken, he had fractured ribs and some of his fingernails were missing. Tracey Connelly prepared for the visit, not by cleaning the house or making sure Peter was clean and dressed. She put chocolate over the bruises on his face and head to disguise them and put cream and chocolate on his hands to cover the missing finger nails.

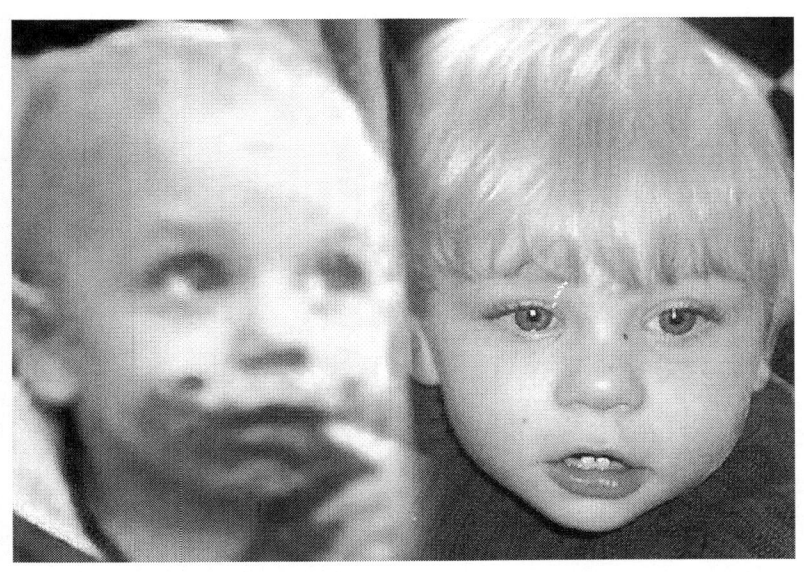

THE HAUNTING PICTURE OF PETER, LOOKING PALE AND GAUNT, FACE COVERED IN CHOCOLATE TO COVER HIS INJURIES, NOTICE THE RED MARKS AROUND HIS EYES.

Peter was placed in a buggy because he was too limp with his broken back to be placed in the highchair. The social worker took a quick look at Peter, but did not spot anything wrong. She said, "Hello, little fella" and that was it. The baby was put in the kitchen, door shut. In the morning, Connelly had actually told the teenage girl that the social worker would have to be "an idiot" not to notice something wrong. If the social worker had just taken a second to look properly, to pick him up and look at him, she would have realized there was something gravely wrong. The next day, Police handed over further reports to the Crown Prosecution Service, including statements from two doctors, saying Peter's bruising was suggestive of "non-accidental" injury. Prosecutors decide there was not enough evidence to bring a case. On August 1st, Peter was taken to a child development clinic at St Ann's Hospital in Tottenham, north London. Pediatrician, Dr. Sabah Al-Zayyat, decides she cannot carry out a full check-up as the boy is "miserable and cranky".

On August 2nd, Peter was left all day upstairs in his cot. In severe pain and hungry, the child was left there crying for hours while the adults were downstairs drinking, smoking, and in the usual routine of television and internet. The crying was nonstop and in the evening Barker said he would sort it out. He went upstairs and shut the door. Barker then punched Peter so hard in the mouth it knocked his tooth out and he swallowed it. Downstairs, they were smiling, as the baby had finally stopped crying.

The next morning, Owens' fifteen year old girlfriend went in to check on Peter. He was lying lifeless in his cot. After eight months of unimaginable torture, Peter was dead. The teenager alerted Connelly, but it would take the mother a further two hours before she called an ambulance. Owen helped Barker get rid of incriminating, bloodstained, bed sheets and went with Barker to dump a bloodstained Babygro in a canal, before fleeing with his girlfriend

The 999 call was made at 11:36 a.m. and it took the ambulance just four minutes to arrive at Penshurst Road. On entering the house, they found Connelly on all fours, crouched over the baby, who was wearing just a nappy. When they picked him up, he was stiff and showed no signs of life. Resuscitation began immediately. Stunned paramedics listened to Connelly as she shouted "oh no, not my baby" as he was taken into the ambulance. They were even more stunned when Connelly demanded they wait so she could go back into the house and search for her cigarettes. Asked whether her child had been unwell his mother replied, "Yes, he was unwell last night, but I didn't bring him to hospital because I get accused of hurting him." After being told Peter was dead, she was heard to cry, "Oh God, don't take away my baby boy; I have been waiting so long for a boy." When the infant's father turned up, onlookers said she appeared "shocked" and kept repeating, "I'm sorry, I'm sorry."

Peter was pronounced dead at hospital after being examined by a team of specialists, then body maps were completed and the Police were called. Connelly was arrested at 13:45 p.m. and taken to Edmonton police station. Peter was reexamined by Dr. Wijemanne, who discovered more than 50 injuries on the infant's body. Along with the broken spine he had injuries which included 8 broken ribs, neck injuries, severed fingertips, missing fingernails and toenails, injuries to his arms and legs, severe head injuries and cut lips.

When police visited Peter's home, they finally met Barker, who told them he was a friend who had been "visiting" that morning. He claimed he knew Connelly from doing "maintenance work". In the Police search of Penshurst Road, they failed to find one piece of Peter's clothing which was not dirty or covered in blood.

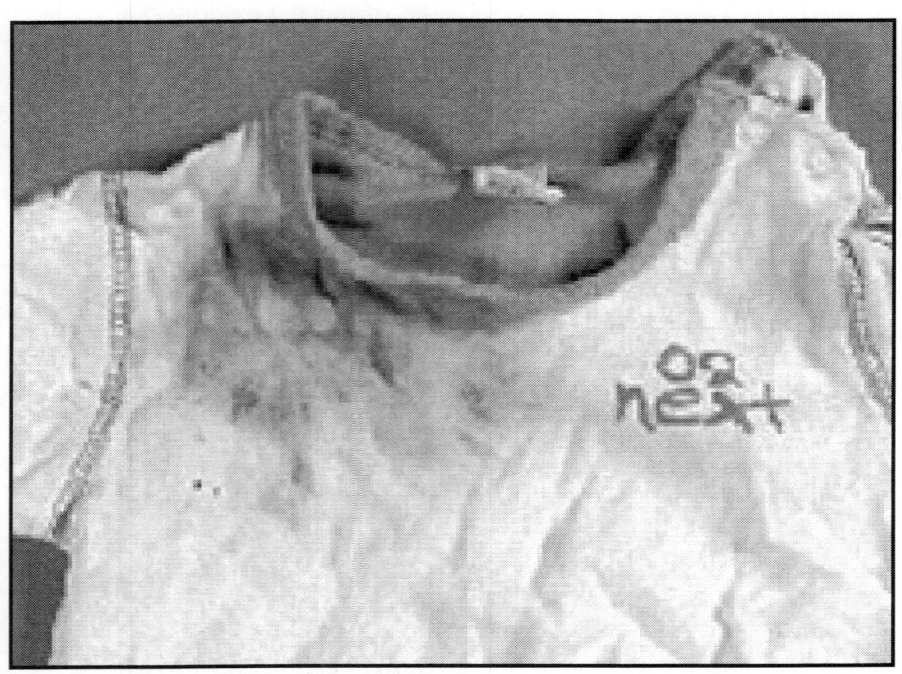

ONE OF PETER'S BLOOD STAINED T-SHIRTS
REMOVED BY POLICE

It was eleven days later when Barker and Owen were arrested in Epping Forest, where they had been hiding out in a makeshift camp. Barker put his survival skills to good use, killing rabbits, which they both cooked and ate. After he was arrested, Barker admitted he had known Connelly for more than two years, but insisted they were "just good friends". Only after a final interview did he admit that they had a sexual relationship and that she was three months pregnant with his child.

While being interviewed, the two men made allegations about each other's involvement in Peter's death. Owen claimed Connelly and Barker had, prior to Peter's death, "wrapped him up like a cocoon and laid him face down on the floor and left him there all day". Barker claimed Owen had gathered the bedding from Peter's cot into a black dustbin liner and disposed of it. Barker told the police that he was scared his brother would try to have him killed if he spoke about him. Owen painted a different picture. He claimed that Barker had tortured their younger brother during childhood. Barker told the police: "I have never laid a finger on Peter ... If anyone says I admitted killing Peter they are lying." He also reacted to an allegation that Owen had found him in the child's bedroom "sweating and excited", saying, "It's a lie."

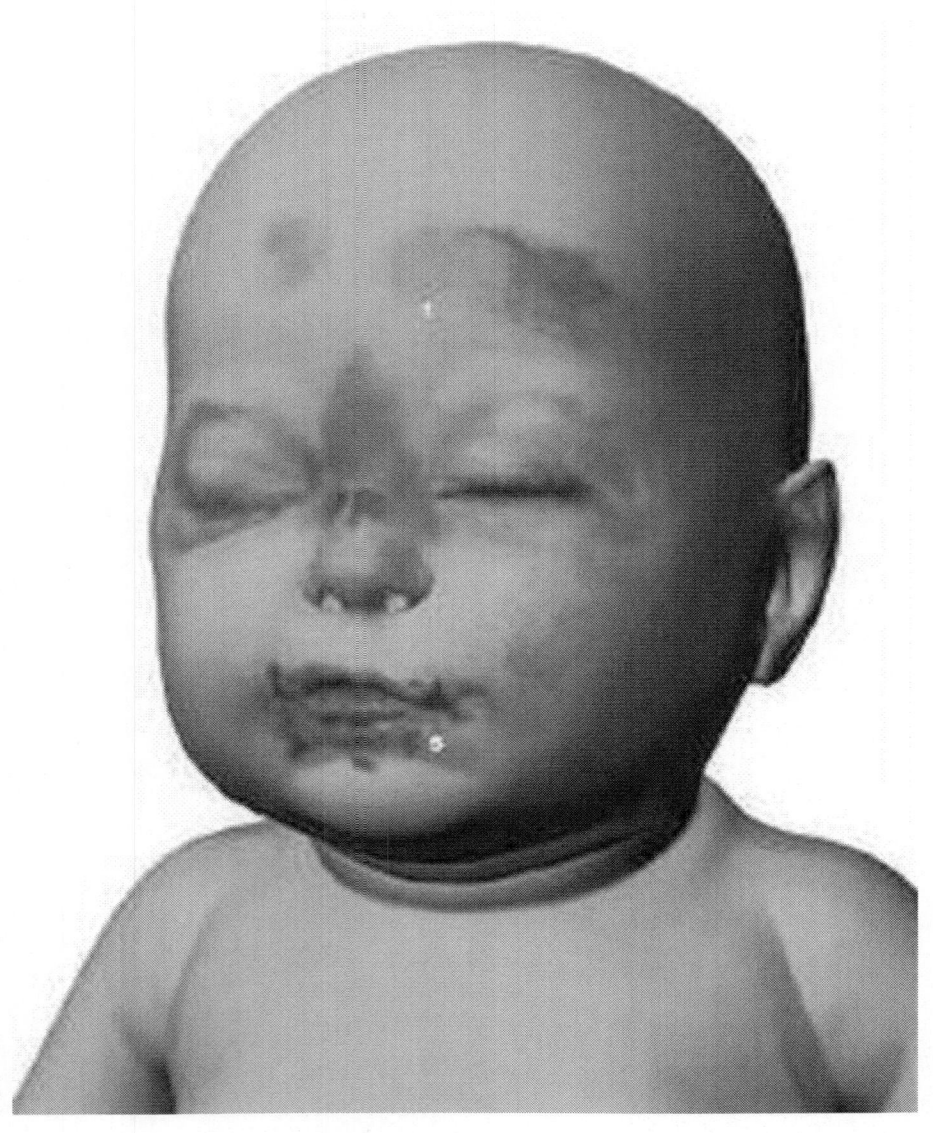

COMPUTER GENERATED IMAGE OF SOME OF THE HEAD AND FACIAL INJURIES ON PETER CONNELLY

A NATION IN SHOCK

THE SHRINE AND TRIBUTE TO BABY PETER CREATED BY THE SHOCKED AND HEARTBROKEN PUBLIC OF ENGLAND

As news broke about Baby Peter's death, a shocked and angry public started to demand answers. Peter was simply known as Baby 'P' for legal reasons. A shrine was soon awash with flowers and tributes left by a heartbroken public. A high court judge made it a criminal offence to name Connelly, Barker, and Owen until a legal deadline had expired, although some internet sites defied the court. The orders were imposed to protect other children in the case and also to avoid prejudicing the upcoming Baby P trial because Barker was being accused of other crimes, including raping a two year old child and child cruelty for which he would be later convicted. The name of the female child he raped will never be publicly revealed but details of her ordeal were told in court when she became the youngest sexual abuse victim to give evidence at the Old Bailey. She provided the courtroom with a heartbreaking narrative, "I was asleep and he woke me up ... he was being naughty ... he pulled his clothes down."

While the mainstream media was forced not to name Connelly, Barker, and Owen, their names and faces were splashed over countless internet sites for months including Facebook, Bebo, and Myspace. More than a million people joined social networking pages which identified them and their names were also circulated in a viral text message sent to thousands of mobile phone users. Defense lawyers seized on the internet campaign as a reason the second trial, for the rape of the two year old should be dropped. They said it would be impossible to find jurors who were unaware of Barker's involvement in the Baby Peter case and argued that any jury would be swayed by the horrific nature of Peter's death. Judge Stephen Kramer QC, who would preside over both trials, insisted it was in the public interest that the trial should go ahead. He ordered that the jury should not be told of Barker's links to Peter, and that he should be tried under a false name, an unusual step normally reserved for gangland 'supergrasses' whose lives were at risk. The judge was forced to halt the rape trial when internet bloggers revealed the false name and full details of the case. An undercover police officer had to be placed in the public gallery at the Old Bailey and Scotland Yard's e-crime unit worked with internet providers to remove offending pages from cyberspace.

From her cell, Tracey Connelly penned a letter to the judge in which she said,

"I'm writing this letter as I am not sure of a better way to express regret. I except I have failed my son Peter for which I have pleaded guilty.

By not being fully open with the social workers I stopped them from being able to do a full job, as a direct result of this my son got hurt and sadly lost his short life.

I'm never going to see my lovely son grow in to the lovely sweet man I believe he would have been.

I have lost all I hold dear to me, now every day of my life is full of guilt and trying to come to terms with my failure as a mother.

I punish myself on a daily basis and there is not a day that goes by where I don't cry at some point".

> Dear Judge
> I'm writing this letter as I'm not sure of a better way to express my regret ▓▓▓▓ I except I failed my son Peter for which I have pleaded guilty.
> By not being fully open with the social workers I stopped them from being able to do a full job, as a direct result of this my son got hurt and sadly lost his short life.
> I'm never going to see my lovely son grow in to the lovely sweet man I believe he would have been.
> ▓▓
> I have lost all I hold dear to me, now every day of my life is full of guilt and trying to come to terms with my failure as a mother.
> I punish myself on a daily basis and there is not a day that goes by where I don't cry at some point.

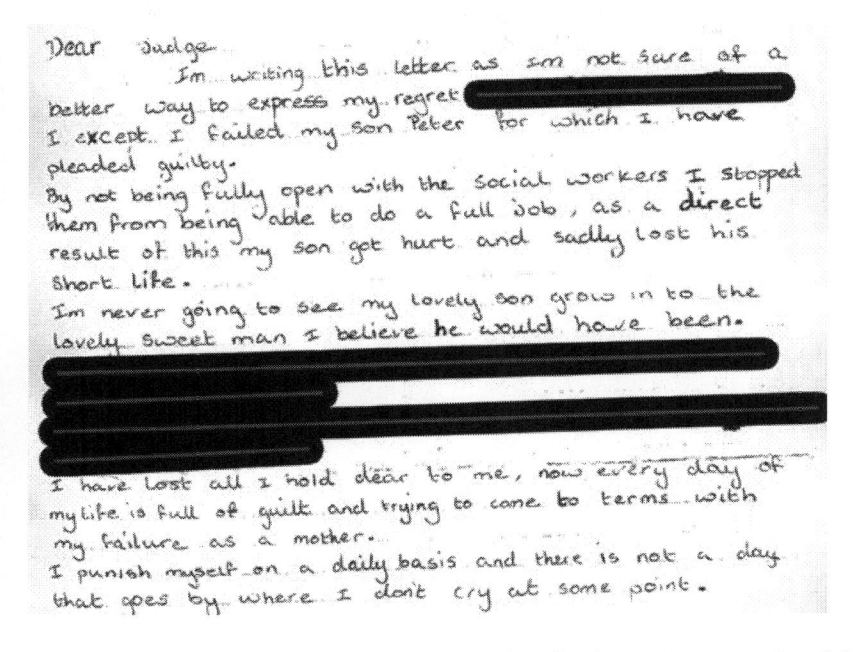

Despite her letter of regret to the judge, Tracey had been penning sickening, self-serving letters to her few friends, insisting she had no idea Barker and Owen were abusing her child. She talked of finding God and wanting to join Peter in heaven, but in the next sentence wrote, "I don't plan to get attached to anyone for a very long time. I'm just going to shag about for a bit and have loads of fun."

None of the three were convicted of murder, the more serious charge that had been leveled at them. Detectives had to admit that the absence of forensic evidence and the lack of reliable evidence from those involved in Peter's last moments meant that they would always have struggled to convict anyone of murder. After deliberation, the Old Bailey judge directed the jury to acquit the three defendants of murder. They were found guilty of an alternative charge of causing or allowing his death. In a bitter irony, this was one of the few decisive acts by anyone in authority dealing with the 17 chaotic months of Baby P's life. Tracey Connelly and Steven Owen were given sentences of minimum jail terms of 12 years and Jason Owen was given an indeterminate sentence of imprisonment for the protection of the public for three years for his part in Peter's death. This meant he could apply for parole after three years but would only be released once the Parole Board was satisfied he no longer posed a risk to the public. Owen challenged his sentence at the Court of Appeal and in October 2009 was ordered to serve a fixed six-year jail term instead. Tracey Connelly also appealed against her sentence but later dropped the appeal.

Owen was named and his identity was released to the press and public as soon as the trial finished but Connelly and Barker kept their anonymity due to the up and coming rape trial. Haringey social services even fought for them to remain anonymous for a period of seventeen years but this was rejected by the high court, which instead set a legal deadline in which they could remain anonymous. Whilst in prison awaiting the rape sentence, Barker was attacked by a fellow inmate at Wakefield prison, where Barker was serving his 12-year jail term. The inmate hurled boiling water at Barker, leaving him screaming in pain. Some reports claimed it had been a concoction of water and sugar, which sticks to the skin and intensifies burns in the same way as napalm bombs. The Ministry of Justice later said no sugar had been involved.

It was reported that fellow inmates applauded as Barker was ambushed. One prisoner gave an insight of what the other inmates thought of Barker, he said, "To say Barker is disliked is an understatement – he is reviled. The other inmates all hate him with a passion. When Barker came here everyone knew what he had done to Baby Peter. Your card is marked if you have a crime against your name concerning kids. After the attack everyone was in good spirits, knowing someone had hurt Barker. The guy who did it will be getting applauded everywhere he goes now. It will be seen as a badge of honor and it is just a matter of time before someone else takes a shot at Barker too." Officers at the high-security jail in West Yorkshire rushed to the scene to calm things down. The inmate said he had been awaiting a chance to strike and went for it when one arose. Owen was so frightened of what would happen when he was released that he was demanding a new identity and even plastic surgery.

Tracey Connelly was oblivious to the fact that she was the most hated woman in the country. She penned letters to her few remaining friends about how she was looking forward to the birth of her new baby and how she was going to have fun when she was released. She befriended infamous serial killer Rose West whilst in prison. Rose West was serving life for her part in the kidnap and killing of several teenagers. Her and her husband Fred had kidnapped and killed several teens, including his own daughter, who they buried in the cellar and back garden of the home.

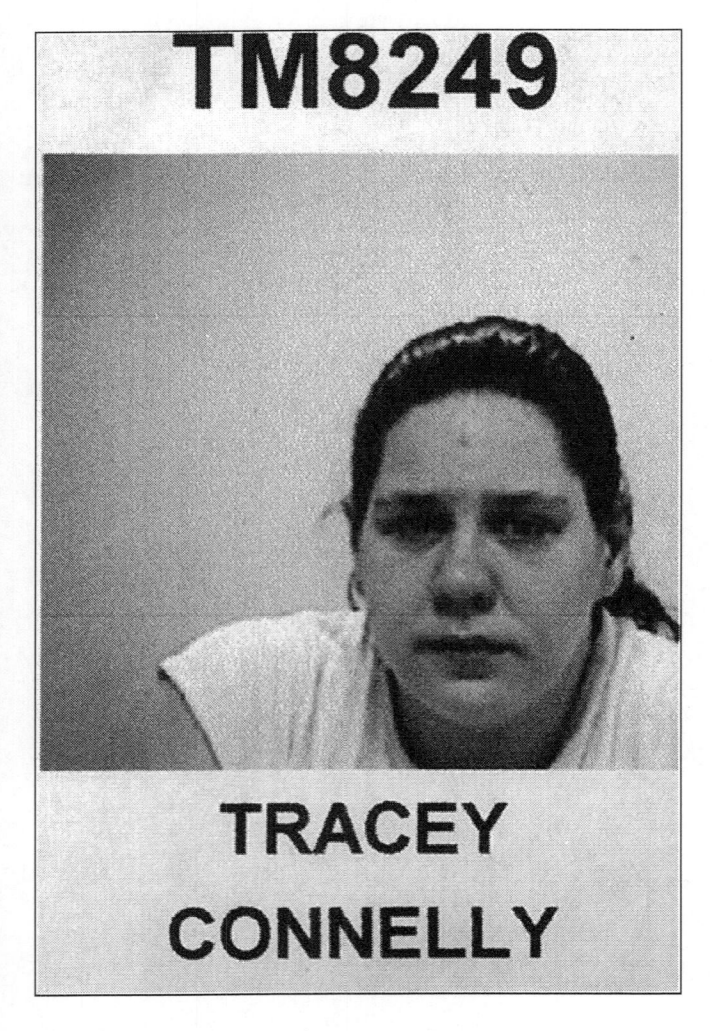

TM8249

TRACEY CONNELLY

The public was outraged that none of the three accused had been convicted of murder and disgusted with the light sentences they received, but with the three safely behind bars, an enraged public and press started to focus their attention on the other culprits, demaning answers and action. In their eyes, the authorities of Haringey council were just as guilty for their part in Peter's death. They wanted the people involved to be held to account.

INEPT, INCOMPETENT, AND GUILTY

As the news broke of Peter's death, labor councilors and social services scurried to hastily arranged meetings behind closed doors. They were aware of the public outrage and that they were about to come under intense scrutiny for their failings. Questions needed answering and the public and press demanded those answers. How could the authorities not have known what was going on after more than sixty visits over 8 months by social workers? Tracey Connelly named Steven Barker, who later battered Peter to death, as her next of kin on health records, so why did council officials fail to investigate his background? Had they done so they would have discovered, through his past that he was a danger to the children.

How could Social workers never realize that Baby Peter was being harmed and how could they have considered his case to be 'a routine, low risk case, requiring family support' and never change their minds? Why? When they knew Connelly, in their own words, was 'disorganized, dirty and smelly' and was 'without much conscience', did social workers fail to confront her? Was it because she 'intimidated the staff'?

Police strongly believed that Baby P's injuries were non-accidental, but why didn't they do their duty by accepting the responsibility to investigate the injuries? They also swallowed Connelly's account of Barker's limited involvement, which showed a 'lack of thoroughness of the police investigation'. Why did the family doctor accept Connelly's lies that he 'bruised easily' when he examined the baby at six months. In the final days of Baby P's life when the doctor said he was in a 'sorry state' why did the doctor not alert others?

Why did social workers accept Connelly's litany of lies about what happened to her child, who she was living with, and who had contact with her children. She said Barker was just a friend and that he was never left alone with Peter. Why did Officials never question her claims? The extent of Barker's involvement with the household was also not known and most importantly his possible criminal background, anti-social behavior or general background, was not known. A man joining a single parent household, who is unrelated to the children, is well established in research as a potentially serious threat to the well-being of the children. He needs to be checked out and his involvement with and relationship to the children carefully assessed. As well as being named as next of kin, Barker went with her to the hospital in April 2007, after Baby P suffered a head injury and he was there when a social worker visited Connelly at home two months later, so why was his involvement not investigated?

The warning signs were there from the start, as, just days after Peter was born, a health worker visited the home and found it to be 'very untidy'. The case was placed in a blue folder indicating it was a cause for concern. So why was Peter still failed until the day he died in a blood-spattered cot? Throughout, why did social workers take a 'sanguine' view of Peter's injuries? Even when doctors took the view that the injuries had been inflicted deliberately, why were these 'discounted'? After attempts to improve how Peter was looked after with a child protection plan proved useless, why did officials then refuse to challenge Connelly's failure to follow it?

In March 2007, just six months before Peter's death, Connelly was seen slapping one of his siblings in the face, in public, 'with very little provocation'. Why wasn't action taken and why weren't police told and why weren't charges pressed? **It gave Connelly the wrong message, that the authorities were not too bothered.** This was not spanking or considered parental discipline but a shocking loss of control directed to the most vulnerable part of a child's body. The police were not informed even though it was a criminal assault. This seemed to reflect the low expectations, which many of the agencies in Haringey appeared to have about families like this.

The following is the full health dossier and all the contact with the authorities that Peter Connelly and Tracey Connelly had from his birth to his heartbreaking death.

2006

1 March: Baby Peter is born.
22 March: Health visitor Yvonne Douglas makes first home visit. Peter has oral thrush.
24 March: Family physician, Jerome Ikwueke, sees Peter for the thrush.
7 April: Yvonne Douglas weighs Peter at baby clinic.
13 April: Six-week examination by Dr Ikwueke.
2 May: Physician visit for diarrhea and vomiting.
4 May: Yvonne Douglas sees mother and Peter at health clinic.
22 May: First vaccinations for meningitis and diphtheria.
28 May: Peter vomiting after feedings. Mother calls out of hours emergency service.
4 June: Physician visit for pain, diarrhea and vomiting.
9 June: Peter's mother seen for depression by mental health worker, Karolina Jamry.
19 June: Physician visit, second immunizations.
11 August: Peter's mother sees Ms Jamry about marital problems.
15 September: Home visit by health visitor Yvonne Douglas.
19 September: Seen by physician for nappy rash.
13 October: Seen by physician for bruising to head and chest. Mother claims this was caused by an accidental fall down stairs.

17 November: Physician visit for upper respiratory tract infection and thrush.
11 December: Peter admitted to Whittington Hospital in north London with bruising to forehead and nose, sternum and right shoulder/breast.
12 December: Peter examined and referred to child abuse investigation team. Peter is seen by DC, Angela Slade.
13 December: Peter examined on ward by consultant pediatrician, Heather Mackinnon.
14 December: Peter examined on ward by Dr Mackinnon.
15 December: Peter discharged into care of Angela Godfrey. A police investigation begins.
18 December: Social worker, Agnes White, visits Peter's mother at home.
19 December: Peter's mother and grandmother are arrested and interviewed at Hornsey police station in north London.
21 December: Peter's leg x-rayed at hospital.
22 December: Peter's mother attends a child protection conference with Haringey social workers and Dr Mackinnon.
24 December: An emergency duty team visits Angela Godfrey's home to check on Peter.
27 December: Social worker, Agnes White, visits P at Godfrey's home and returns later unannounced.
29 December: Agnes White returns to check on Peter's contact with his mother.

2007

9 January: Angela Godfrey takes Peter to health clinic for thrush on buttocks and is seen by Yvonne Douglas.

12 January: Peter's leg is x-rayed again at the hospital.
16 January: Agnes White checks for a second time on Peter's contact with his mother.
17 January: Peter's leg is x-rayed again at the hospital.
19 January: Mother seen by Ms. Jamry.
25 January: Physician visit for nappy rash.
26 January: Repeat visit by Agnes White to check on Peter's contact with his mother, who is seen on the same day by Ms Jamry.
2 February: Peter's third set of vaccinations and Maria Ward assigned as social worker.
8 February: Preliminary assessment of mother by unspecified official, Caroline Sussex.
18 February: Peter and mother moved to new address in Haringey.
22 February: Social worker Maria Ward's first home visit.
27 February: Miss Ward attends case conference at Haringey.
2 March: Miss Ward and health visitor Paulette Thomas visit mother at home.
5 March: Miss Ward questions mother after school nurse sees her slap a child.
6 March: Unannounced visit by Miss Ward.
8 March: Visit by Miss Ward.
14 March: Visit by family support service worker, Marie Lockhart.
16 March: Haringey child protection conference with mother, attended by Miss Ward and Miss Lockhart.
20 March: Mother and Peter videoed at parenting class.
22 March: Miss Ward visit.
23 March: One-year check at health clinic.
29 March: Haringey case conference.

9 April: Peter seen by physician with bruising to face. Mother claims he was pushed into a fireplace by another child. Peter is admitted to North Middlesex Hospital in Enfield, north London, for bruising and swelling to his head.
10 April: Peter referred to child development clinic by a social worker who sees him "head-banging".
11 April: Peter discharged from North Middlesex Hospital.
12 April: Child protection meeting at North Middlesex.
24 April: Home visit by Miss Ward.
3 May: Mother and Peter attend parenting class
9 May: Planned home visit by health visitor, Ms. Thomas.
16 May: Family support visit by Ms. Lockhart.
18 May: Physician visit for hives, an allergic reaction.
21 May: Miss Ward visits.
1 June: Miss Ward makes an unannounced visit and reports Peter's mother to police over bruises to Peter, who is taken to North Middlesex Hospital for a checkup.
5 June: Mother interviewed under caution at Hornsey police station.
6 June: Peter seen by Ms Thomas at the health clinic.
7 June: More immunizations at physician surgery and child protection meeting at North Middlesex Hospital.
8 June: Police take photos of Peter and seize a toy from his home.
12 June: Registered child-minder, Anne Walker, takes Peter for day care for 10 days.
15 June: Home visit by Ms. Lockhart.
19 June: Miss Ward visits child-minder.
20 June: Case conference at Haringey.
21 June: Peter and mother attend a parenting class.

5 July: Mother and Peter attend a parenting class.
9 July: Mother takes Peter to North Middlesex Hospital with an ear infection.
11 July: Home visit by Miss Ward.
18 July: Peter seen at health clinic for a scalp and ear infection.
19 July: Mother and Peter attend a parenting class and go to North Middlesex Hospital about the ear infection.
26 July: Physician visit for head lice and blood in Peter's ear.
30 July: Case conference at Haringey. Home visit by Miss Ward. Mother is feeling stressed.
1 August: Peter seen at St Ann's Hospital in north London by locum pediatrician, Sabah Al Zayyat.
2 August: Mother told police to take no further action over assault allegations.

3 August: **11:36 GMT:** 999 call.
11:40 GMT: Ambulance arrives.
11:43: Ambulance leaves.
11:49: Ambulance arrives at hospital.
12:10 GMT: Peter pronounced dead and police called.
13:30 GMT: Body maps completed.
13:45 GMT: Mother arrested.

LET DOWN BY EVERYONE WHO SHOULD HAVE CARED AND PROTECTED

The first review and report on the death of Peter was completely inadequate. It was overseen by Sharron Shoesmith, the head of Haringey children's services at the time when Peter was being so badly let down by them and at the time of his death. She acted as chairman of the report even though it was her own social workers that were under scrutiny. The summary, published in November of 2008, unbelievably cited 'numerous examples of good practice' in Peter's care. Her review described the relationship between Connelly and her children as 'largely positive'. It highlighted the 'reasonable judgment' used by professionals and praised them for carrying out 'relevant agency checks'. Children's minister Tim Loughton, said of the review that it was complacent and did not get to the bottom as to how many opportunities were missed. Miss Shoesmith told Members of Parliament (MPs) that the outcry over Peter's death was 'absurd'. Ofsted inspectors ruled Miss Shoesmith's review 'inadequate' and she was sacked from her £130,000 a year job. Miss Shoesmith then started legal proceedings against her sacking. Her lawyers argued she was dismissed after Children's Secretary, Ed Balls, allowed himself to be influenced by a "media storm and witch-hunt" over the Baby Peter case.

The Appeal Court concluded that she was unfairly sacked because Mr. Balls and Haringey did not give her a proper chance to defend her case before her removal. The Department for Education and Haringey sought permission to attempt to overturn the ruling in the Supreme Court, but a court spokesman said that their applications had been refused. Mr. Balls said he was "very surprised and concerned" and urged the government to consider changing the law to clarify ministers' powers. He said, "I fear that the Appeal Court judgment will now make it very difficult for ministers to act swiftly in the public interest to use their statutory powers when children are at risk, as I did in this case". The former children's secretary said, "This judgment creates a serious and worrying constitutional ambiguity which now requires urgent action from the government to resolve."

Mr. Balls said that the Ofsted report into Peter's death catalogued "catastrophic management failures" on such a devastating scale that Haringey's council leader and lead member for children's services resigned their posts. "My clear responsibility and duty as Secretary of State was to do everything in my power to keep children safe in Haringey and across the country," said Mr. Balls, "I judged on the basis of that independent report, and on the advice of departmental officials and lawyers, that the right and responsible course of action was for me to use my statutory powers to remove the director of children's services from her position with immediate effect."

Mr. Balls insisted that he had been acting within his powers under the Education Act and in line with the advice of civil servants and government lawyers. Their advice was that it would not be "appropriate" for him to meet Miss Shoesmith to hear her side of the story before removing her from her post. He said, "Ministers need to be able to exercise their legal duties and make judgments in the public interest based on independent analysis and advice. That is what I did and I am concerned that this judgment will make it harder for ministers to do so in future. I believe it is now essential that the Government acts swiftly to resolve this ambiguity, through primary legislation if necessary, to ensure that ministers can act swiftly and within the law when children are at risk."

Asked on BBC Radio Four's Today program if it had been right for her to lose her job, Miss Shoesmith replied, "I'm clearly not going to say yes to that question." She went on, "This is much more complex than saying, 'You are responsible. Let's sack you and the whole psyche of the nation can be at peace'. You cannot stop the death of children. Across the country there are 39,000 children on child protection registers today. As a director of children's services I cannot control what the police do, I cannot control what health does. I cannot control the fact that when a social worker rings to get an appointment at a hospital she cannot get it for four months. I cannot control the fact when a social worker is referring a child for abuse that she rings up and finds that a case has not been allocated to a police officer for four months. I am not in the blame game. I don't do blame."

Jean Taylor, of the victim's group, Families Fighting for Justice, said, "Shoesmith has got to be answerable. She was a public servant, she was put in charge of children's care and she failed. Her attitude shows staggering conceit. It is a downright insult to Baby Peter's name. "She should be ashamed of herself and I think she should simply disappear and not court the media limelight."

SHOESMITH COURTING THE MEDIA AFTER HER APPEAL VICTORY

Dr. Sabah Al-Zayyat was the physician who was supposed to examine Peter two days before his death but did not because she said the baby was cranky and failed to spot that Peter's back was broken and he had several broken ribs. A hospital spokesman said of her failure to examine Peter properly, "Even a junior doctor should have recognized the risks in a situation where there was a letter on file clearly stating there were child protection concerns and the child had visible bruises. The 17-month-old may still be alive today if the pediatric consultant had conducted a full medical examination and recommended that he be taken from his mother. The doctor noticed bruises on him but decided against the examination because he was 'miserable and cranky'. She later said Peter didn't look any different than a child with a cold." Dr. Al-Zayyat was the first person to be sacked in the wake of the scandal when she was dismissed by Great Ormond Street Hospital (GOSH) in May 2008. She was suspended from practicing by the General Medical Council while the investigation took place. Al-Zayyat was employed on a rolling six-month contract by GOSH on a salary of more than £75,000. The doctor, who qualified in Pakistan and worked in Saudi Arabia before moving to Britain in 2004, argued she had been made a scapegoat for wider failures.

The children's hospital, which is a National Health Service (NHS) Trust, runs the child development centre at St Ann's Hospital in Tottenham, where Baby P was brought in shortly before his death. Al-Zayyat claimed that she was never shown the child's full medical history and so did not realize he was the long-term victim of abuse. She started legal proceedings to sue her employer for unfair dismissal. Misconduct charges were brought against her over her treatment of Peter. She was accused of knowing he was on the child protection register, but failing to carry out an adequate examination, failing to investigate the explanation offered for his injuries, and failing to record whether she considered the possibility that he was the victim of child abuse. It was also alleged that Al-Zayyat failed to diagnose that Peter had suffered physical abuse, possible neglect, and emotional abuse, and did not arrange for him to be admitted to hospital.

Dr. Al-Zayyat's hearing was adjourned after a General Medical Council (GMC) fitness to practice panel heard she was 'suicidal', unfit to defend herself. and had left the country. The doctor, who did not attend the hearing, renewed a bid to apply for 'voluntary erasure' of her name from the medical register. The GMC panel granted her request for 'voluntary erasure' from the register, meaning she avoided a full hearing. It also meant that she could still practice outside the United Kingdom (UK). The ruling meant Dr. Sabah Al-Zayyat avoided a full public airing of the very serious allegations against her, to the regret of the GMC, which felt it would be in the public interest. In addition, the panel found she broke the rules by applying for a new job in the Irish Republic without informing the

GMC or telling her prospective new employer about the restrictions on her practice already imposed in the wake of the trial. Many will say she has got off very lightly. Although she won't be able to practice in the UK, there is nothing to stop her working as a doctor elsewhere.

DR. AL-ZAYYAT

Baby Peter's physician, Dr. Jerome Ikwueke, who failed to spot that the toddler was suffering abuse eight days before his death, was suspended for a year for misconduct, but Ikwueke escaped being struck off by a disciplinary panel that had previously ruled there were serious failings in his handling of Peter Connelly's case. He had noticed a marked change in the personality of the previously happy 17-month-old when he was brought to his surgery in late July 2007, observing that the boy seemed 'withdrawn' and pulled away from him. He breached his professional duty to the child by not carrying out a full examination, making an urgent referral for further checks, or sharing information with a health visitor or social workers, the General Medical Council panel found. Peter died eight days after the consultation.

The GMC had already found that Ikwueke's fitness to practice was impaired by his misconduct. In announcing its decision to suspend him from the medical register for the maximum period of 12 months, but not to strike him off, it said that despite the "serious breaches", his failings were "not fundamentally incompatible" with continued registration as a doctor. Although concerned at his "limited insight" before and during the hearing, the panel concluded that the physician did not present a danger to patients in the future, had taken extensive steps to remedy the issues identified, and shown "undoubted remorse".

The chair of the panel, Judith Worthington, said it was necessary to suspend Ikwueke for the maximum period "to maintain public confidence in the profession and to declare and uphold proper standards of conduct and behavior". The panel had previously ruled that he should have considered the possibility of child abuse when he noticed

Peter had bruises on his chest and head at an appointment on October 13 2006, rather than accepting a claim by the child's mother that he had fallen downstairs at "face value". He also failed to mention these injuries when he referred Peter to hospital with further bruising two months later. Worthington told Ikwueke at an earlier hearing: "Your failure towards Peter Connelly was not an isolated incident. It was a series of failures over a period of 10 months and included a number of serious breaches of your professional duty, culminating in your failings on July 26 2007 when Peter Connelly's mother brought him to see you. On that day, his changed demeanor and appearance coupled with all that you knew about his past should have alerted you to the very high likelihood of serious child abuse so that urgent action by you was mandated."

Ikwueke, who qualified as a doctor in Nigeria and worked as a physician for nearly 20 years, denied misconduct. He was supported at the hearing by West Drayton-based physician, Anthony Grewal, who spoke of his "huge personal respect" for Ikwueke and said he would not hesitate to register with him as a patient.

DR IKWUEKE

Maria Ward and Gillie Christou were Peter's nominated social worker and team manager. They were suspended for misconduct. Maria Ward was suspended for two months and Gillie Christou for four months by the General Social Care Council (GSCC). The pair, who admitted failings, had already been suspended from practicing for 16 months during the investigation. Haringey Council sacked Ms. Ward and Ms. Christou, but both launched employment tribunal challenges against their dismissals. At the GSCC hearing, Ms. Ward and Ms. Christou had accepted they did not ensure Baby Peter was visited enough; they lost contact with him for a time, and did not keep adequate records. The GSCC ruled that the women should not be struck off the social care register.

GSCC committee chairman, Jonathan Roberts, said it had decided not only that "such a course was disproportionate to the facts admitted at this hearing", but also that such action would have been "to satisfy a perceived public demand for blame and punishment for a registrant who does not present a continuing risk". Mr. Roberts added that mitigating factors, taken into account, included the women's admissions of the allegations against them, their otherwise unblemished records, the staff shortages and excessive caseloads at the council at the time, and the fact that Baby Peter's mother was a "skilled and manipulative liar".

Peter's death was "an eminently avoidable tragedy", said Marios Lambis, counsel for the GSCC, who told the hearing that the social workers' efforts had been "ill-focused, naive and inadequate". Nick Toms, counsel for the pair, said that both women "deeply regret" what happened to Peter and had been "devastated" by the case. "Their reputations will probably never recover from the battering they have received in the media," he said.

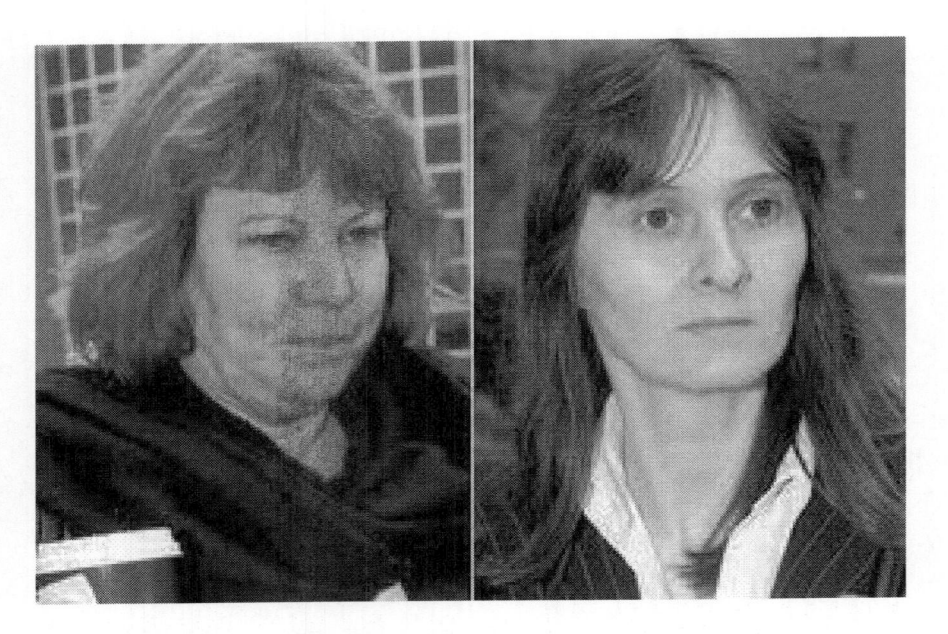

GILLIE CHRISTOU AND MARIA WARD

A SICK PAIR OF MONSTERS

If any more proof was needed as to what sick, twisted monsters Steven Barker and Tracey Connelly were it came at the trial for which Barker was accused of raping and sodomizing a two year old girl. The sadistic 32-year-old Barker was found guilty after the girl became, at the age of four, the youngest rape victim in legal history to give evidence. The girl was attacked by Barker while she was supposedly being monitored by Haringey Council. This is the same London borough which also failed Baby Peter and an earlier victim of abuse, Victoria Climbie. Psychiatrists warned that Barker would always be a danger to children and police investigated concerns that he abused two other girls. An independent investigation began into how he was able to target the girl, seemingly under the nose of the local authority.

The girl's harrowing account was at the center of the trial and without her key evidence; the prosecution could not have gone ahead. The rape victim, who cannot be named for legal reasons, was placed on Haringey's child protection register in December 2006 over fears she was at risk of neglect. The social workers in contact with her family had no idea she had been targeted by the same pain-obsessed brute who tortured Baby Peter. She was later taken into foster care, and told her foster mother that Peter's stepfather had sexually abused her. Police and social services were called, but when detectives asked the girl, then aged three, if the man had touched her she shook her head, and the investigation was dropped, potentially wasting a vital chance to investigate.

Two months later the child made the accusation again and re-enacted the alleged rape to child psychiatrists, using a doll and a teddy bear to show what had happened. A doll and a teddy bear were the only way the little girl could communicate what had happened to her. She placed the doll on its stomach on a dolls' bed, and then placed the teddy bear face down on top of it, before telling a child psychiatrist that the man had hurt her when she was just two. "It was not nice what he did," she said, "He hurt me. It hurt all day." The little girl's haunting account of what happened to her, given when she was only three, was recorded on video and played to the Old Bailey.

After the court saw the video, the child was subjected to a 45-minute cross-examination. For this, she was sitting with an adult in an Old Bailey annex, which was linked to court by video camera. Her obvious distress and tough questioning at the hands of two defense lawyers raised disturbing questions about how the criminal justice system deals with very young witnesses. Dr. Michele Elliott, of children's charity Kidscape, said, "This adversarial way of questioning children was outrageous. Of course a barrister can confuse a four-year-old. She will have found it a searing experience." Barbara Esam, of the NSPCC, said, "Some children who have not been properly prepared for the impact of giving evidence have gone on to show psychological and physical symptoms, including self-harming, bed-wetting, and trouble at school." The cross-examination left the girl so upset that she later called the video room where she gave her evidence "the evil room". The Crown Prosecution Service did not oppose the decision to allow her to be questioned because her testimony was the basis of the case. Without her there would have been no prosecution.

It was November 2007 when she first told her foster care

parent that the man had touched her. She was two at the time. When a female detective asked if she had been abused, the girl shook her head signifying a "no" answer. It was two months later; during a meeting with child psychiatrist Margaret DeJong that she gave a full account. During that meeting in January 2008, she made a series of startling revelations, saying she "hated" Baby P's stepfather and that he had hurt her. Dr. DeJong told the court, "She said 'He hurt me with his willy'. She said it happened lots of times. She said she had told him to stop but that he never did." Police gave her a full medical examination. A video of the subsequent interview was played to the courtroom in which the giggling three-year-old played 'shops' and even hide-and-seek with police. She told police, "He hurt me. I was sleeping, he woke me up... He was being naughty again... I was in my 'jamas (pajamas). He was lying down... like penguins do." Asked if she had said anything to him, she replied simply that she had said, "Don't do it." The girl was Connelly's daughter.

For the cross-examination the judge and lawyers removed their horsehair wigs before speaking to her. She answered their questions through the video link.

Bernard Richmond QC, who defended Peter's stepfather, asked her if she understood 'fibs'. Mr. Richmond asked her to remember her November 2007 police meeting when she shook her head when asked about abuse. The girl fell silent when the defense lawyer asked her why this was so. Mr. Richmond persisted, firing questions at her until, finally wrong-footed, she appeared to give the answer he wanted. "He never touched you, did he? Did he?" the barrister asked. There was silence in the courtroom until, moments later; she gave a tiny shake of her head.

Her almost imperceptible response was seized upon. "Was it something someone told you to say? Was it something you made up?" Mr. Richmond asked. After a long pause she replied: "I just...." and then fell silent again.
Mr. Richmond said, "I have to ask you one more time, he didn't touch you, did he? We have to have an answer; he didn't touch you, did he? I have to wait until I get your answer, so I can't ask any more questions. He didn't touch you, did he?"

After a five-minute break, Mr. Richmond then continued, asking the child, "What is truth?" She grew upset, wiping her face with her hands, and the barrister was unable to get any further answers. Paul Mendelle, QC, defending Connelly, saw his questions met by nods, shrugs and silences from the little girl. Prosecutor Sally O'Neill QC said the girl had simply been confused by their complex questions, and was too upset to describe her ordeal. Police feared her courtroom experience may have caused her untold psychological damage, on top of the trauma of the rape itself. A senior police source said: "We hope this will trigger a re-examination of how young witnesses are handled. It's something we will push for."

Barker was sentenced to a life term with a recommendation he serve a minimum of ten years. Barker appealed the conviction and the sentence. But his challenge was rejected by the Court of Appeal in London. He claimed his conviction for the rape of the two-year-old girl was "unsafe". Barker's QC, Bernard Richmond, had argued at the hearing that an Old Bailey judge should have halted the case against him. The argument put forward to the appeal judges by Mr. Richmond was that the evidence of the girl should have been excluded. The trial judge, he submitted, should have ruled that the child was not a 'competent' witness. Lord Chief Justice, Lord Judge, said the child "was indeed a compelling as well as a competent witness". He added, "On all the evidence this jury was entitled to conclude that the allegation was proved. Unless we simply resuscitate the tired and outdated misconceptions about the evidence of children, there is no justifiable basis for interfering with the verdict."

Lord Judge said both Baby Peter and the rape victim, referred to only as X, were "exceptionally vulnerable by reason of their ages and the appellant's activity represented a gross breach of trust". He added, "All the reports upon the appellant indicate that he is a danger to young children. He committed appalling crimes." A spokesman for the Crown Prosecution Service said it was pleased with the judgment, adding the victim "demonstrated extraordinary courage". "Those who abuse children should remember that their victims are not too young to help secure a conviction," he added. Lord Chief Justice, Lord Judge, Lady Justice Hallett, and Mrs. Justice Macur, also dismissed Barker's appeal against his sentence. Barker's dramatic conviction in the rape case meant the ban on reporting the trial was lifted. As a result, Baby P was named for the first time as Peter, at the request of his real father, the report into his death said it could have been prevented, and Haringey issued a groveling apology over its failures to protect the children.

Tracey Connelly had faced a charge of cruelty in relation to the rape, but was found not guilty by the jury of eight men and four women. The girl told the Old Bailey that Connelly walked in during the sex attack, but made no attempt to stop it or to rescue her. The victim claimed Connelly had only turned to Barker and wagged her finger at him, telling him, "Don't do that... Don't do it." Detectives believed the convicted child rapist may have sexually abused the two-year-old girl at least three times in 2007, before his arrest over Peter's death in August 2007. But he was only charged with a single count of rape, because lawyers feared it would be too difficult for his young victim to try to give evidence about several different occasions.

BEYOND BELIEF

Tracey Connelly gave birth to a daughter while on remand at Holloway prison, and in a move which was beyond belief, social workers wanted her to keep the baby and have time to bond. Police intervened and the child was soon taken into care, put up for adoption and given the chance of a better life. Prison was a comfort for Connelly and she piled on the weight, eating chocolate, watching television, and taking part in the odd pottery class. In a letter to a friend a month after being sentenced, she was still oblivious to her crimes, "I have never been the best mum in the world, but I'm not the worst and I'm not the sort of mum who would hurt her children." Denying that she knew what Barker had done, she said, "as the weeks and months passed I slowly started to wake up to the truth, so now I hope he rots in hell". The failed mother was already planning a party for when she got out of prison. She wrote to the friend, "I tell ya, when I get out, I'm in no rush to get in a relationship with a man again, but I might have fun playing the field and travelling (one long party!). Hope you're going to join in the party." In another, she wrote, "I would love to visit Egypt and Greece and Rome. I would love to see the pyramids and go down the Nile."

Just days before she was publicly named, she was moved from Holloway to Low Newton, near Durham, where she had been placed in solitary confinement for her own safety. There was a massive backlash against Tracey

Connelly when her identity was made public. Quickly after she was transferred to Low Newton, she became a target for other inmates who found out she was there. She was swiftly transferred to 460-inmate Styal Women's Prison in Cheshire, but news of her arrival caused similar outrage among prisoners. Connelly revealed in letters to a friend that despite being widely condemned following the death of her 17-month toddler, that she had received no fewer than six marriage proposals since the start of her prison sentence. Connelly who had already served a third of her five year jail spell, boasted of the proposals saying, "I have had some strange letters, including six men asking me to marry them. Needless to say I binned the letters!!" She had also revealed how she was improving her culinary skills, including mastering the recipe for a pizza base along with some memorable jam tarts. Connelly wrote, "I did make some lovely jam tarts the other week and I learned how to make pizza dough a few weeks back. Prison life is very slow and almost every day is the same, but unlike most wings we are allowed to cook our own meals. Some of us love to bake cakes when it's a birthday we treat each other a lot. At the moment I'm about 19-and-a-half stone (273 lbs.) as I put on a lot of weight when I came to prison."

Tracey did express some remorse when she wrote, "I wish I could turn back the clock and change things, but I can't do so, all I can do is look to the future and hope for the best. It is very painful to talk about as I failed my son. I'm trying to get my head back together. I hope in time I will learn how to forgive myself but it will take a lot of time and a lot of counseling." As for Barker, she insisted that she could never forgive him despite him claiming that his sins have been pardoned since becoming a Jehovah's Witness. She wrote, "As for Steven saying God forgives him, well I truly hope God does forgive him as I know I never can. Thing is, I hate him. If I'm honest, I wish I didn't hate him it means I still think of him. I want to feel nothing for him. My future plans are just to prove myself as a person so I can get out."

The evil mum of even boasted of her "joy" at getting prison visits from her children. She gloated about the visits in one of the letters, writing that her 11-year-old eldest daughter "hasn't changed much" and is still "bossy". Connelly, was allowed to see the children twice a year while she served the rest of her sentence. The person who received the letter about the visits from her children said, "It's sickening how she talks of her kids but never Peter. It's like he never existed. Tracey constantly says how much she loves the girls, but it's hard to listen because of what happened to Peter and she thinks she can continue where she left off with her kids when she gets out, but she can't. She likes spending time with them as they don't know what the rest of the world knows about her, maybe because they're too young. To them she's still mum. Sadly, one day they'll learn what she did." In the letter, Tracey also revealed she had been doing Bible studies and has begun an Open University degree.

If there was ever a female who should never be allowed anywhere near a child ever again it surely has to be Tracey Connelly. She is up for parole in 2012 and petitions have already been circulated to keep her in prison.

JUSTICE NOT DONE

On the 5th of August 2011, Jason Owen walked out of jail, a free man. The monster left Wandsworth Prison in southwest London early in the afternoon. His release came just two days after the fourth anniversary of tortured 17-month-old Peter Connelly's shocking death. Owen had served just over two years in prison. He did not receive the new identity or face lift he had demanded whilst serving his sentence. He was released to a bail hostel in London. Newspapers put appeals out to members of the public to tell them where Owen was. He was seen strolling in a park amongst mothers and children, the same age as Peter would have been had he lived. He was then spotted on an outing from the probation hostel for high risk offenders casually walking down the street in smart new clothes; he looked relaxed, slim and fit. On his right arm was a tattoo with the provocative slogan 'Only God can judge me'. He had thrown himself into an extreme fitness regime behind bars, including runs of as long as eight miles. He now bears little resemblance to the scruffy, bloated and hollow-eyed police mug shot taken in 2007. The release of Owen is the latest painful injustice that has characterized the case. Baby Peter was failed by the authorities at every turn.

OWENS SICK TATTOO

FOREVER REMEMBERED

Peter Connelly will never be forgotten, neither will the monsters and authorities who were responsible for his death. Internet tribute sites still receive thousands of tributes, poems and messages of love from people all over the world. A jumbled collection of teddy bears, toys and flowers are the only indication of the final resting place of the child. Every year at Easter, Christmas and on his birthday, tributes are left and he is shown the love he sadly missed during his short life.

Baby Peter's ashes were placed, by his father, in a quiet corner of a London cemetery, at the foot of an oak tree, resplendent in its autumn colors. Where the ashes of Baby P are scattered, there exists a tribute to a child whose short, tortured life has touched the heart of a nation. There's no gravestone and no plaque. Baby Peter's father is said to have intentionally left the spot unmarked so that none of the people involved in his death would be able to visit his grave. However, there is a memorial of teddy bears that shows an affection which was absent in his 17-month-old life. He lived a life which was brutally ended by those who were meant to care for him.

TRIBUTES TO AN ANGEL

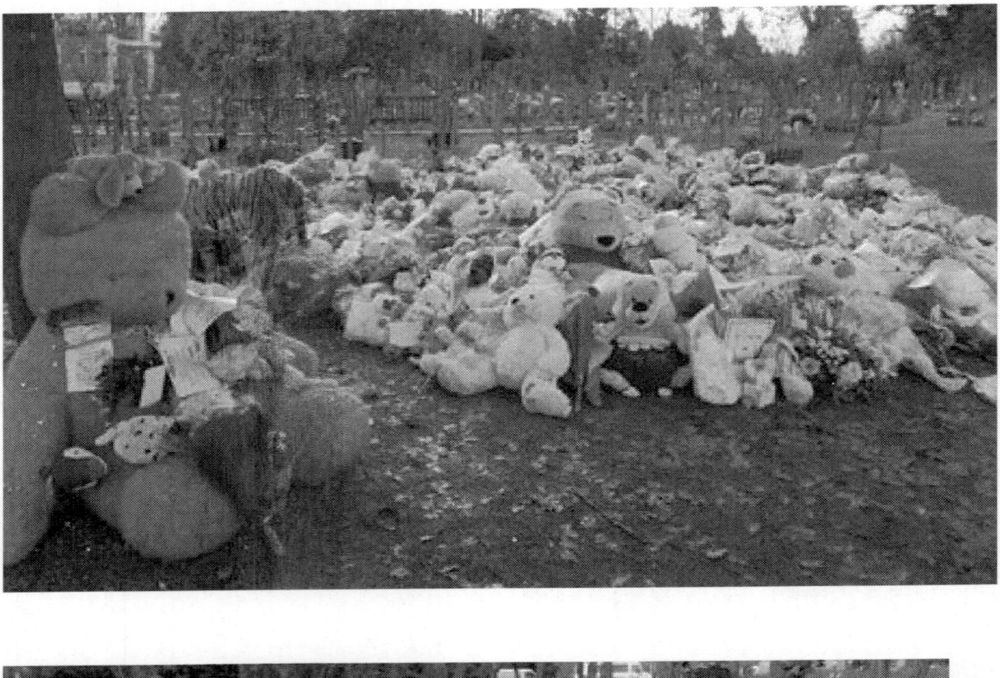

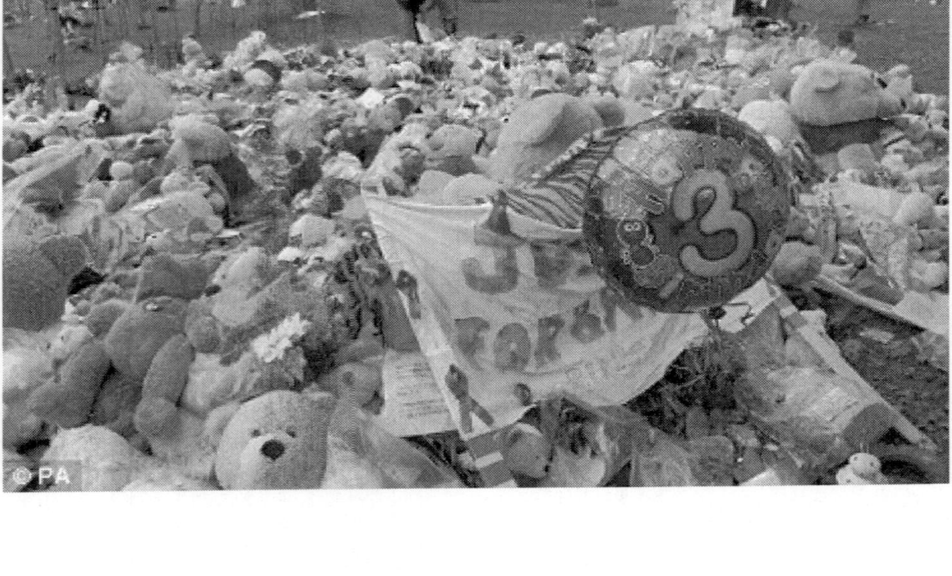
© PA

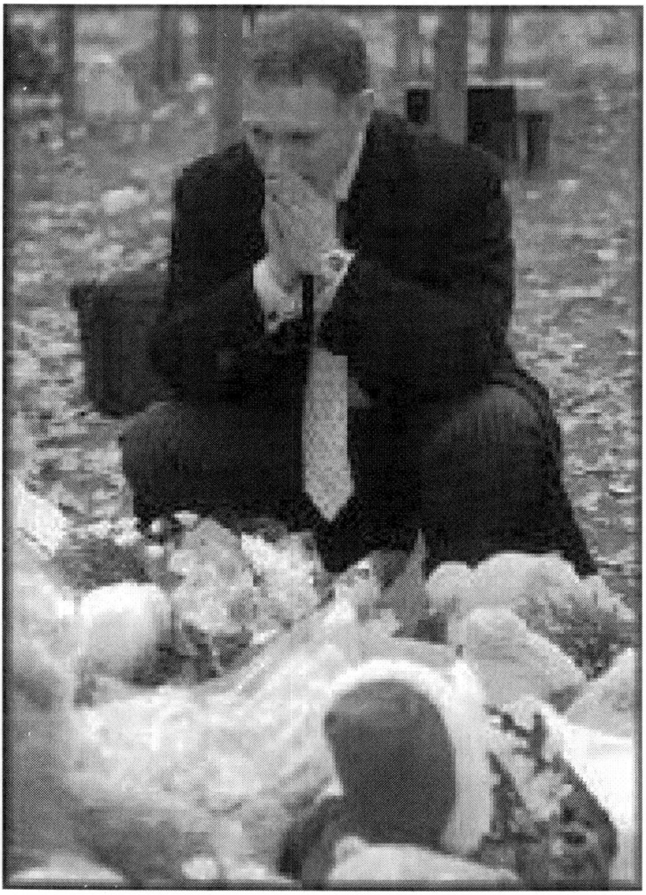

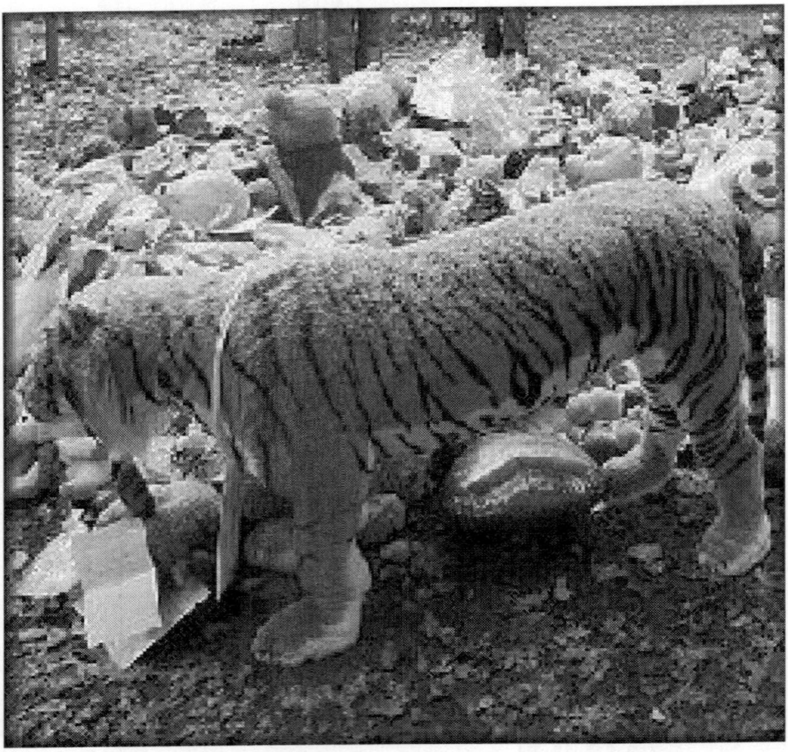

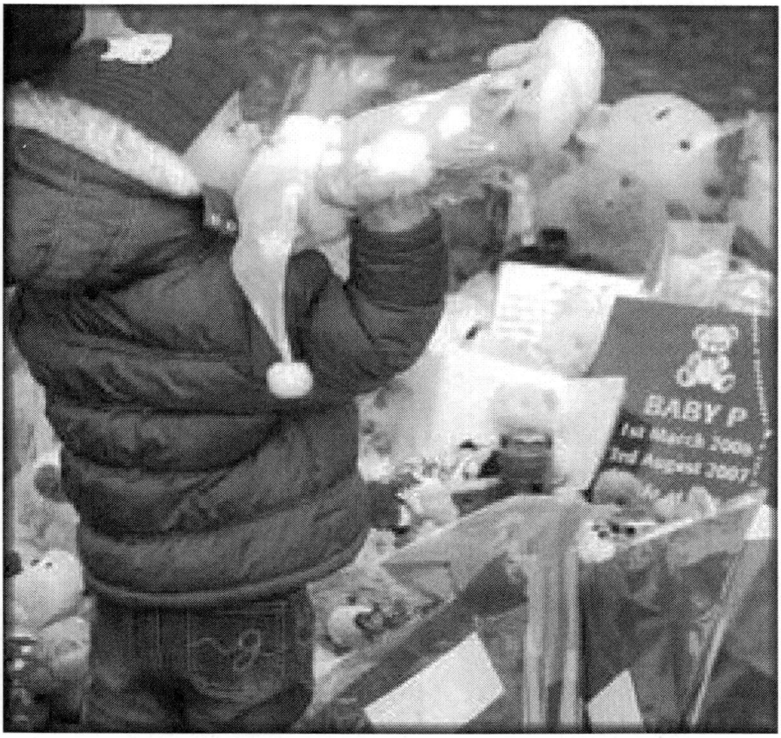
BABY P
1st March 2006
3rd August 2007

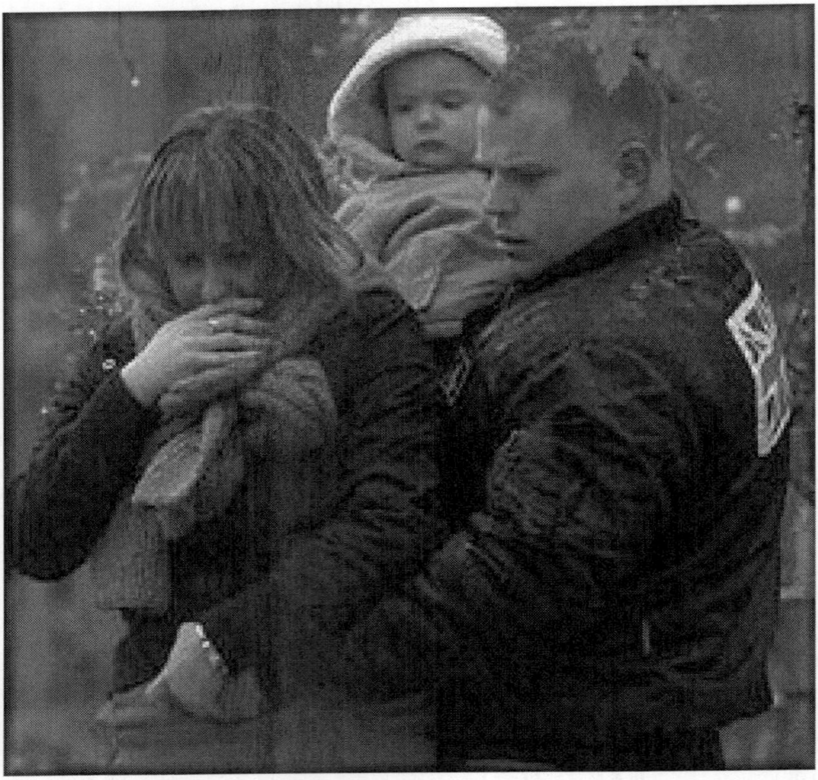

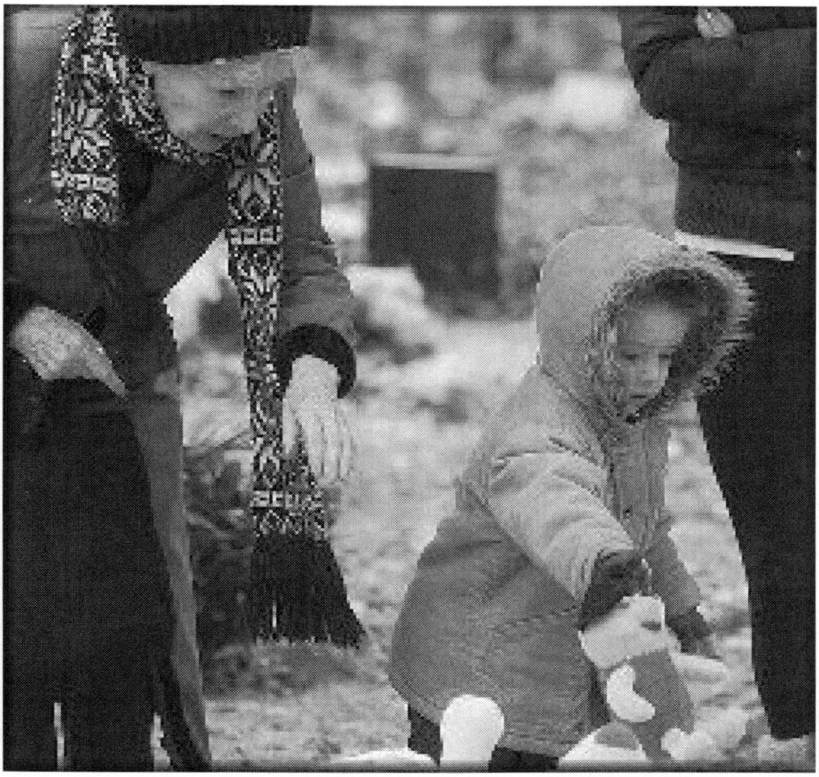

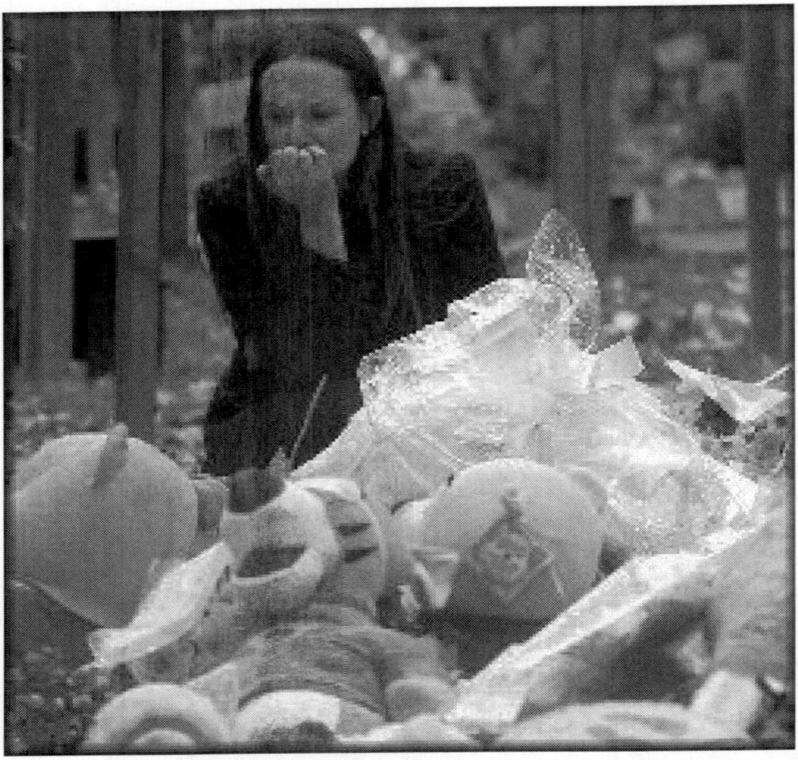

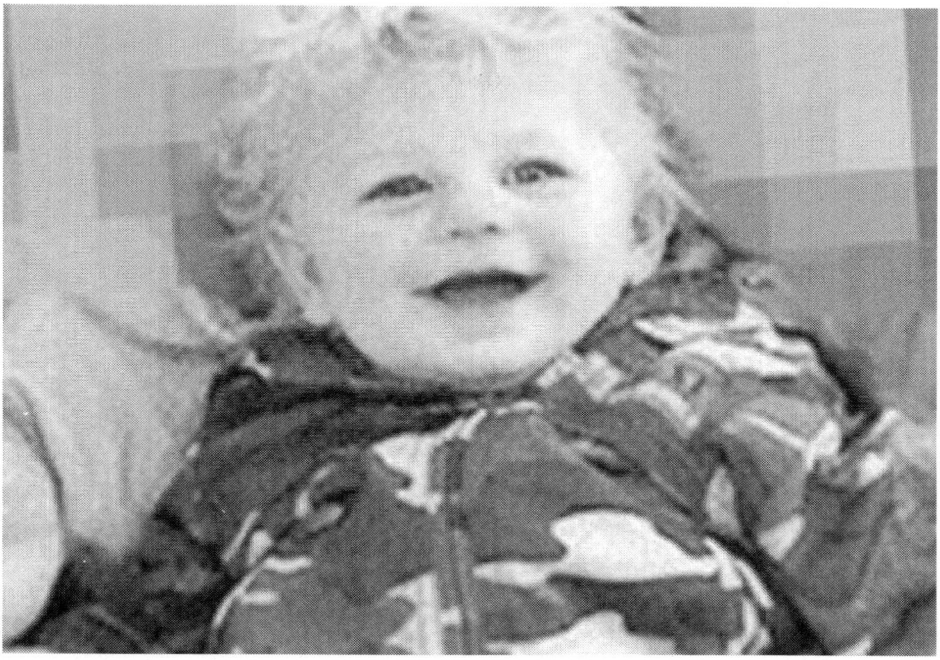

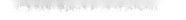

Printed in Great Britain
by Amazon.co.uk, Ltd.,
Marston Gate.